She Fights Like Heaven
A Devotional for Daughters Who Forgot They're Dangerous
Cynthia Oliver

Whispers & Warfare

Contents

Dedication

To my daughter, you carry our legacy of faith like a flame in the darkness. You stand in your God-given identity, unshaken by the storms of life. I'm proud beyond words to watch you rise in holy boldness, and my heart bursts with love as I see you stand as both a gentle heart and a fearless warrior, and one incredible mama. You have taught me that the battles I fought were not in vain, for you will fight on with that same bold fire.

To my best friend, Kristi, my soul sister forged not by blood but by battle, our bond was born on our knees in prayer where we have wept and warred together against the darkness. You have held up my arms when they grew weary, and you have celebrated each victory as if it were your own. We have truly learned the meaning of spiritual authority, wielding our prayers like swords and our laughter like medicine. My heart swells with gratitude for your unwavering friendship.

For Sonya. Your battle is over... Your victory secured...We will see you again one day. Of that I am assured.

Preface

IN THIS DEVOTIONAL, I place a mantle of courage upon your shoulders. Wear it as daughters of THE KING, clothed in strength and dignity, armed with love and spiritual authority. Let this be our war cry and our intimate song of thanks: that we were born for such a time as this, to stand together, hearts ablaze, unyielding. Now I charge you, RISE UP beloved warriors, and FIGHT LIKE HEAVEN!

Introduction

This is not your typical devotional.
This is not your sit-down, be-sweet, cross-your-legs,
paste-on-a-smile, "good vibes only" kind of journal.
This is HOLY WAR paint.
A battle cry in 30 days.
A sacred reminder that you were never meant to be silent,
small, or sidelined.
You were made to RISE, ROAR, and RECLAIM.

Somewhere along the way, you forgot who you were.
You traded your sword for survival.
You let the fight wear you down instead of train you up.
You believed the lie that gentle meant weak, and that
strong meant cold.
But sis, You are BOTH Strong and Gentle.

This devotional is for the woman who feels too bruised to be brave.

Too broken to be used.

Too tired to show up.

Too afraid to take up space.

This is for the woman who needs to remember that she is NOT just loved,

SHE'S ARMED.

Over the next 30 days, you're going to dig deep.

You'll cry. You'll fight. You'll rest.

You'll scream-worship in your car and whisper prayers on the bathroom floor.

And through it all, you'll rediscover that GOD didn't just save you,

HE SENT YOU.

So, grab your journal, your Bible, and your battle playlist.

Because you're not just going to get through this season.

You're going to TAKE BACK GROUND.

This isn't about becoming stronger.

It's about remembering YOU ALREADY ARE.

Let's fight like Heaven.

Day 1

The Lie of "Too Much" and "Not Enough"

*"For we are His workmanship, created in Christ
Jesus for good works, which God prepared
beforehand so that we would walk in them."
Ephesians 2:10 (NASB)*

Some days you just walk into a room unsure of which version of yourself
you are going to be. Some days you just feel like **too much**.
Too emotional. Too intense.
Too bold. Too loud. Too opinionated.
Too soft. Too passive. Too much to handle, yet somehow never quite enough
to be chosen, kept or loved the way you long for.

Other days you feel like **not enough**.

Not spiritual enough. Not holy enough.

Not pretty enough.

Not disciplined, successful, strong enough.

Just lacking.

This is the cruelest kind of lie, the one that swings like a pendulum.

And somehow, the enemy convinces you that both lies can be true at once.

That you're somehow **both too much and still lacking**.

So you shrink.

You edit yourself.

You apologize for the space you take up.

You become quieter, smaller, safer, thinking that maybe then you'll be enough.

But here's the truth:

You were never meant to be palatable.

You were meant to be powerful.

God didn't create you in moderation.

He made you **on purpose, with purpose, and for a purpose.**

He called you *His workmanship*, not His mistake.

And the moment you stop wrestling with the world's expectations,

you'll start walking in the power of your God-given identity.

The world may hand out labels like warnings. But the Kingdom gives

you a name. **DAUGHTER. CHOSEN. BELOVED. EQUIPPED. DANGEROUS.**

You are not "too much." You are **anointed.**

You are not "not enough." You are **handpicked and Heaven-approved.**

And the only one who should be uncomfortable with your fire is

the one who tried to extinguish it.

Identity Reset Prayer:

Father,

Today, I reject the lies that say I'm too much or not enough.

I am exactly who You created me to be, no edits, no filters, no fear.

Let me walk in my full identity chosen, cherished, and commissioned.

I'm done shrinking. I'm done striving.

Let me be so full of who You say I am, that there's no room left for insecurity.

In Jesus Holy Name,

Amen.

Song Reflection: "You Say" by Lauren Daigle

"I keep hearing voices in my mind that say I'm not enough,"

Let this anthem breathe truth back into your spirit.

Let every note speak louder than the inner critic.

Listen until His voice becomes the loudest one in the room.

Journal Prompts:

When was the last time you felt like too much or not enough? Who told you that?

What parts of yourself have you been hiding, editing, or shrinking?

Write a new identity declaration, starting with: "I am not too much.
I am not lacking. I am _____."

Day 2

Loved Loudly, Not Barely

"I have loved you with an everlasting love;
Therefore I have drawn you out with kindness.",
Jeremiah 31:3 (NASB)

THERE'S A VERSION OF love this world hands us that feels like
crumbs.

Conditional.

Unstable.

Earned.

Something you have to perform for, Apologize for.

Cling to like it'll slip away if you breathe wrong.

And if you've been hurt long enough, you start to believe that's all you're

worth. So when someone says, "God loves you," it lands a little flat.

Because if love's been a battleground your whole life, how are you supposed

to believe it's your safe place?

But here's the kind of love you were actually made for:

Loud.

Unshakeable.

Undeniable.

Relentless.

Real.

Not the kind that ghosts you in silence or leaves you questioning your value.

Not the kind that makes you small or scared or second-guessing.

But the kind that walks straight into your mess without flinching.

The kind that stays.

That fights. That covers. That heals.

You are not barely loved.

You are extravagantly pursued.

God didn't whisper love in your direction, He declared it from a cross.

He doesn't love you because you're perfect.

He loves you because <u>**He is**</u>.

You don't have to earn it.

You don't have to chase it.

And you never, ever, have to beg for it.

You are already the one He wants.

Already the one He called.

Already the one He died for.

So stop settling for crumbs when Jesus broke Himself to give you the whole table.

His love :

Crossed Heaven for you.
Hung on a cross for you.
Dances over you.
Declares " Nothing can separate you from My love"
Thats not halfway. That's not bare minimum. That's loud.
All in. Louder than shame. Louder than fear. Louder than lies.
You were meant to be loved loudly.

Unfiltered Prayer:

Jesus,

I've spent too long trying to earn what You already gave.

Trying to shrink myself into someone worth loving.

But You love me fully. Loudly. Honestly. Always.

Help me believe that. Help me receive that.

I don't want love I have to chase, I want the kind that found me first.

And that's You.

Let that be enough for me.

In Jesus Name

Amen.

Song Reflection: "Pieces" by Amanda Cook / Bethel Music

"You don't give Your heart in pieces. You don't hide Yourself to tease us."

Let this one undo you a little. Let the lyrics undo what people broke.

Let your heart learn to trust again, because **He never loved you halfway**

Journal Prompts:

What has shaped your view of love, parents, partners, pain?

Where have you settled for less than the kind of love God offers?

Write a letter from God to your heart, starting with: "My love for you has never been quiet..."

Day 3

Built from Dust, Crowned in Grace

"Then the Lord God formed the man of dust from the ground and breathed into his nostrils the breath of life...", Genesis 2:7 (NASB)

You were built from dust.
Not diamonds. Not marble. Not gold.
Dust. Dirt. Earth. Fragile. Raw. Real.
And still, He called it good.
He looked at dust, breathed into it, and saw destiny.

So let's stop pretending we were made to be flawless.
Stop holding our breath trying to look polished and perfect
When our very origin story started with dirt under the nails
of God's own hands.

You weren't created to be untouchable, you were created to be **formed**.

Molded. Grown. Seen. Loved, even in the mud.

And crowned while still messy.

Because that's what grace does.

It doesn't wait for you to be shiny before it calls you chosen.

It doesn't wait for the wounds to close before it calls you worthy.

It sits with you in the dirt and whispers,

"Even this is part of your becoming."

Let's get honest: you've got dust.

The past, the pain, the shame, the shattered pieces.

But He's not afraid of any of it.

In fact, He's still forming beauty from it.

You are not what you've been through.

You are not the dirt you've walked through.

You are dust, yes, but you are divine dust.

Formed by the breath of God.

Crowned with grace.

Covered in purpose.

Crowned in grace means that you don't have to climb to be chosen.

You don't have to shine to be seen.

You don't have to be flawless to be favored.

Grace doesn't wait for you to "arrive." It meets you in the wreckage,

wraps its arms around your weariness, and whispers, "You're mine."

Grace is not afraid of your mess. It doesn't walk away when you doubt.

It is the holy hush in the chaos, the unexpected beauty in broken things,

the scandalous truth that even dust can be royal when Heaven declares it so.

You were made from the mess. And still, you carry the mark of royalty.

So remember when you feel like you're crumbling again,
Even Dust Still Belongs to Him

Redemption Prayer:

God,

Thank You for not needing perfection to call me Yours.

Thank You for making beautiful things from dust, like me.

Breathe on the parts of me that feel dry, cracked, lifeless.

Remind me that grace doesn't wait for me to have it all together.

It finds me right here, dirt-stained, tear-streaked, and still worthy.

In Jesus Name,

Amen.

Song Reflection: "Beautiful Things" by Gungor

"You make beautiful things out of the dust. You make beautiful things out of us."

Let the truth of this song dig deep.

You are not disqualified. You are in process.

And **God DOES NOT waste dirt.**

What "dust" in your life have you been ashamed of?

What would change if you believed God could breathe on it and bring life?

Write a prayer of surrender for the messy parts of your story you've been hiding.

Day 4

Still Here, And That's A Miracle

"But God, being rich in mercy, because of His great love with which He loved us, even when we were dead in our wrong doings, made us alive together with Christ...", Ephesians 2:4–5 (NASB)

You almost didn't make it.
And I don't just mean once.
You almost didn't make it through that heartbreak.
That loss.

That grief.

That desperation.

That breakdown behind closed doors.

That season where it felt like God went quiet and grief got loud.

You had days where the weight on your chest didn't lift.

Where the silence felt like punishment.

Where brushing your hair and getting out of bed felt like warfare.

And yet, **you're still here.**

Not untouched.

Not unscarred.

But **still here. Still standing. Still His.**

That's not weakness. That's *a miracle.*

Sometimes we wait for the breakthrough to celebrate.

But sis, the miracle is that you *didn't break.*

You didn't quit.

You didn't walk away from faith even when you wanted to.

You didn't let bitterness win, even when it begged to.

You kept showing up, even if all you could do was whisper His name.

So maybe today isn't about being the strongest in the room.

Maybe it's about saying:

"God, I'm still here. And that means You're not done."
Let that be your anthem.
Let that be your worship.
Because survival isn't small, it's sacred.
And the breath in your lungs is proof that the enemy *lost again.*
Thats exciting isn't it?
It deserves a dance of victory (even if it is in your secret place.)
Let's be honest.. we all do our victory dance in our secret place.

Breath-of-Grace Prayer:

God,
I almost didn't make it, but You kept me.
I wanted to give up, but You never let go.
So today I won't despise the scars,
I'll call them survival stories.
Thank You for every breath I thought I'd never take.
Thank You that even on my weakest days, I was never out of Your reach.
You kept me. And because I'm still here, I know You're still working.
Thank you, God, for your fresh breath of grace
In Jesus Name
Amen.

Song Reflection: "Rescue"by Lauren Daigle

Let it play. Let the words hit.

"I will send out an army to find you in the middle of the darkest night."

You were not forgotten in the fight.

You were rescued. And you're still here. That's holy ground.

Journal Prompts :

What is one moment you thought you'd never survive, but did?

How can you celebrate your survival story today, even if you're still healing?

Finish this sentence: *"I'm still here, and that means..."*

Day 5

When Her Quiet Is Still Powerful

"In returning and rest you shall be saved; in quietness and trust is your strength.", Isaiah 30:15 (NASB)

Not every warrior walks in loud.
Not every fighter is the one with the mic or the spotlight.
Some of the most dangerous women to hell are the ones who fight **in silence, on their knees, in rooms no one sees.**

She's the one who prays in the car between errands.
The one who cries into her pillow and still shows up for others.
The one who doesn't post about her battle, but lives through it anyway.

She doesn't need to shout to be strong.
Because **Heaven doesn't measure strength in volume, it measures it in surrender.**

Her quiet is not weakness.
Her quiet is filled with fire.
Because her strength isn't in how loud she can be, it's in **how deeply she trusts.**

When the world says, "Be louder,"
God whispers, "Come closer."

There's something sacred about stillness.
It's where clarity returns.
It's where anxiety loses its grip.
It's where God does some of His best work.

And if you're the quiet one, let me tell you this:
Don't mistake your softness for smallness.
You're not invisible. You're intentional.
And your stillness? It's *spirit-shaking*.
Keep showing up.
Keep trusting, even in the dark.

Because even in silence, **you are still a storm to the enemy.**

Let that sink in.. Soak in the quiet and know that even in
the quiet
He is speaking. In your silence you can hear His voice.
Sometimes you have to be still, to hear that small voice, to
receive
an outpouring of grace.

Stillness Prayer:

God,

The world says to hustle, but You tell me to rest.

You say strength is found in stillness.

So I come back to You, not with noise, but with need.

Thank You for being the God who sees the quiet ones.

The ones who fight without applause.

The ones who war in whispers.

Let my quiet trust move mountains.

Let my stillness be a weapon.

In the name of Jesus,

Amen.

Song Reflection: "Speak the Name" by Koryn Hawthorne (feat. Natalie Grant)

This one's for the whisperers, the ones who fight with quiet faith and steady fire.

Even if your voice shakes, **your spirit doesn't.**

And the name of Jesus still answers your quietest prayer.

Journal Prompts :

Have you ever felt like your quiet personality made you less impactful?

Why?

What battles have you fought silently that deserve to be honored?

What does stillness look like for you, and how can you make space for it this week?

Reflections

How are You Feeling?
Check in

Identity Check-In:

You've reclaimed who you are. Not who the world said you had to be. Not what fear tried to rename you.

Who do you know yourself to be now, after 5 days of truth- telling?

What lies did you break agreement with?

What name is God calling you that you're finally ready to receive?

Prompt :

Write a "Dear Me" letter from the version of you who now knows she is called, covered, and crowned.

Day 6

The God Who Sees the Girl Behind the Strong Face

"You are the God who sees me...", Genesis 16:13
(NASB)

You've been strong for everyone.
Holding space, carrying burdens, smiling through the
storm.
You know how to show up.
You know how to stay steady.
You know how to say, *"I'm fine,"* even when your heart is
cracking
like glass beneath your ribs.

Maybe you lead the room, run the meeting, manage the kids, check in on

your friends. And nobody asks how you are.

Because they assume you are always okay.

But here's the truth:

Being the strong one gets heavy.

And sometimes you wonder, *is anyone seeing me the way I see everyone else?*

You've learned to hold it together so well that you

don't know how to let yourself fall apart.

Not in public.

Not in front of the people who need you.

Not even in front of God sometimes, because even your prayers feel tired.

When Hagar was alone, used, dismissed and running away, God fund her in

the wilderness and said, " I see you." Not just the runaway, Not just the

servant. The person. The heart. The daughter.

And He sees you, too.

Not the version you curate, the girl underneath.

The one behind the strong face.

The one who's tired of being strong.

He saw Hagar in the wilderness.

He saw the tears that never hit the floor.

He saw the strength it took to get up again, and again, and again.

And He sees you.

Fully. Tenderly. Fiercely.

You don't have to be the strong one today.
You can be the seen one.
The held one.
The *loved* one.

Let Him meet you behind the mask.
Let Him carry what you've been too exhausted to keep holding.
Because the God who holds the universe doesn't expect you to hold it all, too.

Honest Prayer:

Abba Father,

You see the me behind the strong face.

The version of me I don't show anyone.

The one that's tired. The one that's doubting.

Thank You for not needing me to be okay to be close.

I'm tired of being the strong one.

I want to be the *surrendered* one.

Meet me here, in the middle of the mess I hide.

I know You won't flinch.

In Jesus Name

Amen.

Song Reflection: "You Know Me" by Steffany Gretzinger

This is the one to play when your mask is slipping, and your heart is raw.

Let the words be a balm: *"You know me... and You still love me."*

There's no version of you He doesn't already love.

Journal Prompts :

Who do you feel like you always have to be "strong" for?

What would it feel like to let that armor drop, even for a minute?

If you could be completely honest with God right now, what would you say?

Day 7

Scarred but Set Apart

*"From now on let no one cause trouble for me,
for I bear on my body the marks of Jesus.",*
Galatians 6:17 (NASB)

You don't come through a storm without scars.

You don't walk through fire and emerge without some smoke in your lungs.

You don't cry on the bathroom floor night after night and come out untouched.

But somewhere along the way, you were taught to hide the evidence.

To tuck the trauma into polite conversation.

To smile over the stitch marks and silence the story.

To swallow our own discomfort with a smile and keep moving forward.

So you've got scars.

Some visible.

Some internal.

Some from what they did.

Some from what you survived.

Some from the battles no one saw but God.

Sometimes we view our own scars as a sign of defeat.

We are ashamed to let them show. Ashamed of how they got there.

Afraid that if people saw them, they would see ugly.

Because if people saw your scars, maybe they'd question your worth.

Maybe they'd think you're too broken.

Too complicated.

Too wounded to be used.

But listen to me:

Your scars don't disqualify you.

They prove you made it.

They're not ugly. They're sacred.

They are the receipts of a war you didn't die in.

They are the proof that the enemy tried, and failed, to take you out.

Jesus didn't hide His scars.

He *showed* them.

Because redemption doesn't erase the pain, it reclaims it.

You are not less holy because you've been hurt.

You are not less usable because you've been through it.

You are scarred, but you are set apart.

And if the enemy wants to come for you again,

all you have to do is hold out your hands and say,

"My God has already bled. You already lost.

My scars are my victory."

Reclamation Prayer:

Jesus,

Thank You for redeeming the parts of me that still ache.

Thank You that my scars don't shame me, they mark me as Yours.

I release the fear of being seen as "too much."

I release the lie that I have to hide my history to be used by You.

You didn't waste Your scars, and You won't waste mine.

Use them. Use me.

Heal others through them.

Let them shine with glory, not shame.

In Jesus Name

Amen.

Song Reflection: "Scars" by I Am They

Let every lyric remind you:

"I'm thankful for the scars, 'cause without them I wouldn't know Your heart."

Don't hide the evidence of God's deliverance.

Those scars shine with survival

Journal Prompts :

What scars, physical, emotional, or spiritual, have you been trying to hide?

How has God met you in the places where you've been wounded?

Write a short testimony that starts with: *"I thought that would destroy me. But instead..."*

Day 8

His Voice Over My Overthinking

"My sheep listen to My voice, and I know them, and they follow Me.", John 10:27 (NASB)

Your mind is loud.
It reruns conversations. Rehearses worst-case scenarios.
It fills in silences with fear.
It overanalyzes what they meant when they said *that*.
It looks like a broken record on the moments you wish you could undo.

Overthinking doesn't ask for permission,
it sets up camp and calls itself "prepared."

But it doesn't bring peace. It brings pressure.
It clutters your clarity.
And before you know it, you've mistaken anxiety for discernment,
fear for wisdom, and spiraling for strategy.

But God isn't shouting over your chaos.
He's not the voice of guilt.
He's not the "what if" or the "you should've."
He's not the endless loop.
He is the *still, small voice* that whispers:
"I know the way. Just follow Me."

You don't have to figure it all out.
You just have to follow.
His voice is steady. Gentle. Firm. Clear.
And it's the only one that leads to peace.

So next time your mind gets loud, pause.
Don't rush to fix it.
Don't overanalyze it.
Just ask:
"Is this voice leading me to peace, or to pressure?"
And follow accordingly.

Clarity Prayer:

God,
My thoughts are loud, but You are louder.
Not in volume, but in truth.
Silence the lies.
Still the storm in my head.
Let me hear You above the noise, above the spiraling, the striving,
the overthinking.
When I can't figure it out, help me to follow the sound of your voice.
Your voice is my anchor. I trust it to lead me home.
In Jesus Name
Amen.

Song Reflection: "You Already Know" by JJ Heller

Let this song be the exhale you didn't know you needed.
"Everything around me seems uncertain,
My weary heart can't take much more surprise..."
And yet, **He already knows.**
And He's already leading you forward

Journal Prompts :

What thoughts have been running on repeat lately?
Are they true or just loud?

What's one situation where you've overthought yourself into exhaustion?

Write down 3 statements you know *God* would say to you today, no filters, no fear.

Day 9

Tear-Stained Prayers Still Reach Heaven

"You have taken account of my miseries; Put my tears in Your bottle. Are they not in Your book?", Psalms 56:8 (NASB)

SOME PRAYERS DON'T COME out pretty.

They don't sound poetic.

They don't quote Scripture.

They're messy. Raw.

Croaked out between sobs and gasps.

Sometimes they don't even make it out as words, just a *"God, please."*

And still, He hears them.

Not just hears them. He holds them.

Your tears are not lost.
They don't evaporate.
They don't hit the floor and disappear unnoticed.
He bottles them.
Counts them.
Writes them down.

You've prayed through heartbreak, prayed through silence,
prayed when you weren't even sure if it was working.
And still, those prayers moved Heaven.

Don't let anyone convince you that a broken prayer is a wasted
one.
Don't let shame silence your cry.
Because **some of your most powerful moments were the ones
no one saw.**

God's not looking for polished.
He's not impressed by performance.
He responds to your honesty.
And nothing is more holy than the moment you let your guard
down,
fall at His feet, and just let the tears fall.

He's not uncomfortable with your pain.
He's the *only One* who can turn it into purpose.

So cry if you need to.

Sob. Collapse. Breathe slow.
And pray with the kind of realness that makes hell nervous.

Because every tear is a testimony in the making.

Held Prayer:

Jesus,

Thank You for collecting every tear I've ever cried.

For hearing the prayers, I was too tired to finish.

For answering the ones, I didn't even know how to pray.

I lay it all down again, the grief, the disappointment,

the aching hope. I trust You with my sorrow.

I trust You with my story.

Even when I'm falling apart, I'm falling into You,

because I know that you will catch me.

In Jesus Name

Amen.

Song Reflection: "Hope in the Hurting"
by Cross Timbers Worship

Let this one sing over your soul.

"When my hope is fading, when my strength has reached the end.."

Every tear. Every prayer. Every piece.

Held. Heard. Loved.

Journal Prompts :

What prayer have you been afraid to say out loud, because it hurts too much?

When was the last time you felt fully honest with God? What held you back?

Write a letter to God that starts with: *"Here are the tears I haven't let fall yet..."*

Day 10

Called While Crushed

"We are afflicted in every way, but not crushed;
perplexed, but not despairing; persecuted, but
not abandoned; struck down, but not destroyed.",
2 Corinthians 4:8–9 (NASB)

YOU'RE STILL CALLED.
   Even though you're tired.
   Even though you're grieving.
   Even though there are days you question if you're really "the one"
God meant to choose.

You don't feel qualified, you feel crushed.
The kind of crushed that doesn't just press you, it *shapes* you.

Because you've been walking through the fire and still showing
up
like it doesn't burn.

And somewhere in the middle of the pain, you started to
wonder:
Can I really be called if I'm still bleeding?
The easy answer is:
YES!
You can be **crushed and chosen.**
Wounded and anointed.
Bleeding and delivered.
Tired and still terrifying to the enemy.

Because calling doesn't require perfection, it requires
presence.
God isn't waiting for you to be flawless.
He's just waiting for you to say yes, even with shaky hands and
a bruised heart.
In the crushing is when he is preparing you, directing you.
The oil comes from crushing.
The anointing is often born in affliction.
And your "*yes*" while bleeding carries a weight in Heaven
that your comfort never could.

So no, you're not broken beyond purpose.
You're not disqualified.
You're not late to the plan.

You are **right on time, right in the fire, right in the middle of His will.**

Still called.
Still chosen.
Still dangerous

Fire-Through-The-Fracture Prayer:

God,
I don't feel strong, but I say yes.
Even in the crushing. Even when I don't understand.
Use my pain for purpose. Use my wounds for Your glory.
Remind me that I'm not disqualified, I'm *being refined.*
Crush what needs to go.
Pour out what You're pressing inside of me.
And let oil flow from this breaking.
In Jesus Name
Amen.

Song Reflection: "Refiner"by Maverick City Music

This one is *raw*. It'll wreck you in the best way.
Let your soul sing, even if it's trembling.
"I wanna be tried by fire, purified... take whatever You desire,
Lord, here's my life."
Even in the crushing, your calling hasn't been canceled,

it's being cultivated.

Journal Prompts :
What have you walked through recently that's made you question your calling?

How has your pain deepened your purpose, even if it doesn't make sense yet?

Finish this declaration: *"I may be crushed, but I am still called to _____."*

Intimacy Over Performance:

You stopped performing.
You came closer.
You got real.

What shifted when you realized God wanted your presence,
not your perfection?

What was the hardest moment to be vulnerable, and what did God show you there?

What rhythm of rest, prayer, or silence do you want to carry forward?

Prompt :

Create a "Sacred Space" list, 3 things you can do this week to stay in the
secret place with Jesus.

Day 11

Daughter, Not a Doormat

"See how great a love the Father has given us, that we would be called children of God; and in fact we are.", 1 John 3:1 (NASB)

You were never meant to be the one everyone walks on just because
you carry grace.
You were never called to shrink just to make someone
else feel more secure.

You are a daughter of the King, **not a doormat for people's dysfunction.**

Yes, Jesus calls us to serve.
Yes, He calls us to forgive.
But never once did He call us to *lose ourselves* trying to keep other people comfortable.

You were made to love, *not to be used.*
You were made to show grace, *not to carry abuse.*
You were made to lay your life down in obedience,
not in burnout, bitterness, and silence.
You are not less holy because you have boundaries.
You are not less kind because you say no.
You are not less Christ-like because you decided to stop bleeding for people who kept handing you the knife.

God never asked you to be small so others could feel big.
He called you daughter.
That one hits to good.. I have to say it again.
He called you daughter.
And daughter doesn't mean quiet, apologetic, or invisible.

It means *loved.*
It means *protected.*
It means *chosen.*
It means *you get to walk in rooms like you belong there, because you do.*

So go ahead and straighten your crown.

Reclaim your seat at the table.

And stop apologizing for standing tall in the name of the One who raised you from the ground up.

You are a daughter of the MOST HIGH KING.

That is no small thing. That makes you royalty.

Let's face it, who doesn't want to be a princess?

Royal Prayer:

Abba,

I've spent too long letting people walk all over what You died to redeem.

I want to love like You do, but I don't want to lose myself in the process.

Teach me to serve with strength, not self-erasure.

To walk in humility, not humiliation.

To live like a daughter, NOT a doormat.

In every room I enter, let me remember **I belong to You.**

And that makes me royalty.

In Jesus Name

Amen.

Song Reflection: "Who You Say I Am" by Hillsong Worship

Let it rise up in you, truth that doesn't just sound good but feels *true* again.

"I am chosen, not forsaken, I am who You say I am."

Let that daughter identity sink in until you walk like it, speak like it,
and **fight like it.**

Journal Prompts :
Where have you mistaken people-pleasing for godliness?

What boundary do you need to set that honors both God and your worth?

Write this in your journal (and mean it):

"*I am a daughter, not a doormat. I can serve without shrinking.*"

Day 12

Wielding the Word Like a Sword

"Take the helmet of salvation and the sword of the Spirit, which is the word of God.", Ephesians 6:17 (NASB)

Let's sharpen the steel and go *straight into battle mode.*
This one's for every woman who forgot that her
Bible isn't just a book,
it's a **weapon.**
You've been swinging with your fists.
Fighting battles in your mind.

Trying to will your way through it with grit, self-help quotes, and deep breaths.

But baby, **you were not meant to fight empty-handed.**

God gave you a sword.

Not just for comfort. Not just for coffee table aesthetics.

But to *cut through lies.* To *slice through confusion.*

To *stand your ground when hell tries to shove you off your purpose.*

The Word isn't just a book.

It's a blade.

And when you open it, memorize it, declare it, you're swinging.

Every promise is a strike.

Every truth is a counter attack.

Every verse is a reminder that *you don't just survive this fight, you win it.*

But here's the thing about a sword:

It only works if you pick it up.

Not once a week. Not just when you're desperate.

Daily. Faithfully. Fiercely.

This isn't a gentle read.

This is how you train.

This is how you fight like Heaven.

You don't need to know the whole Bible; you just need to *use what you've got.*

So start with one verse. Speak it out loud.

Declare it over your home, your heart, your head.

You're not just quoting Scripture.

You're clashing with darkness and coming out blazing.

Battle Prayer:

Lord,
Let me fall in love with Your Word again,
not out of duty, but out of desperation.
Let me wield it like a weapon.
Not just read it, but *fight* with it.
When the enemy whispers lies, let truth be my sword.
When fear surrounds me, let Scripture slice through the fog.
Train my hands for war.
And let Your Word be my first response, not my last resort.
In Jesus Name
Amen.

Song Reflection: "Surrounded (Fight My Battles)" by Upper Room

Let it rise in your spirit like a battle cry:
"It may look like I'm surrounded, but I'm surrounded by You."
Grab your sword. Speak the Word. **You fight different now**

Journal Prompts :

What's a lie you've been believing that needs to be cut down by truth?

What verse can you memorize this week and declare over your situation?

Finish this sentence:

"When I speak God'sWord, I'm not just reading, I'm_____."

Day 13

You Can Be Soft and Still Slay

"Your gentleness makes me great.", Psalms 18:35
(NASB)

This isn't a cute line, it's a quiet rebellion.
A holy contradiction. A reminder that the world doesn't get to
define strength
by volume or victory by aggression.
Somewhere along the way, you were told you had to choose:
Be strong or be soft.
Be fierce or be feminine.

Be bold or be kind.

Somehow the world has convinced you that to lead, to last, to be taken

seriously, you would have to be louder, sharper, tougher.

And so you started to armor up.

You learned how to be tough.

How to guard your heart.

How to never let anyone see the tears.

Because softness got mistaken for weakness, and

gentleness got labeled as passivity.

But **what if you can be soft and slay?**

What if gentleness is actually a *power move* in the Kingdom?

Jesus flipped tables, but He also washed feet.

He roared with righteous anger and whispered to the broken hearted.

He wore both strength and softness without apology.

It's Esther fasting in silence before going to the king.

It's Mary sitting at Jesus's feet while others scurried to impress.

It's Jesus weeping at Lazarus's tomb, right before commanding

death to loosen its grip.

Softness isn't a lack of power. Its a choice to wield it differently

The world says "dominate" .

God says "serve."

The world says "defend yourself."

God says "let Me fight for you."

You don't have to harden to survive.

You don't have to silence your tenderness to be respected.

There is *holy power* in a woman who knows when to speak fire
and when to speak healing.
There is warfare in compassion.
There is strength in kindness.
There is divine confidence in the woman who doesn't need to shout
to shake the room. You can hold someone's hand, speak gently, forgive
first, stay kind, and still dominate in a boardroom, and tear down walls
the enemy spent years building.
Let the world keep telling women they have to pick one lane,
you were made to walk in both.

You are soft.
You are strong.
You are sacred.
And you slay in the Spirit, not in spite of your softness, but *because of it.*

Prayer for Dual Strength:

Jesus,
Thank You for showing me how to carry both strength and softness.

Help me unlearn the lie that I have to be hard to be holy.
Let my gentleness shake the atmosphere.
Let my tenderness be a weapon that heals.
Let my kindness not be mistaken as weakness.
Give me wisdom to know when to roar and when to rest.
I don't want to perform strength, I want to embody it.
In Jesus Name
Amen.

Song Reflection: "Kind" by Cory Asbury

"You are not who I thought You were, kind, patient, and full of grace..."

Let this song soften your heart again.

Let it remind you that gentleness is a fruit of power, not the absence of it.

You can be kind. And you can still take down giants.

Journal Prompts :

Where have you felt like you had to "toughen up" to be taken seriously?

What part of your softness do you want to reclaim today?

Write a truth statement:

"I am soft, and that means I am _____."

Day 14

Beauty Isn't Her Superpower, Obedience Is...

*"Charm is deceitful and beauty is vain, but a
woman who fears the Lord, she shall be praised.",*
Proverbs 31:30 (NASB)

Let's flip the whole table.

Because today's entry is for every woman who's been measured
by
how she looks instead of how she moves in the Spirit.

You've been told your power is in your reflection.
Your curves. Your skin. Your hair.
The way you dress.
The way you pose.
The way you present yourself to the world.
 And it's exhausting.

Because deep down, you know this truth:
beauty fades, but obedience endures.

Your superpower isn't how you look in the mirror.
It's how you move when Heaven speaks
The enemy isn't scared of your selfie, he's scared of your "*yes*".
Your surrender.
Your conviction.
Your obedience in the secret place.

That's what shifts atmospheres.
That's what tears down strongholds.
That's what builds legacies and breaks generational curses.

Beauty may open doors, but obedience walks through them
and
changes everything on the other side.
There's nothing wrong with being beautiful.
But don't ever let anyone convince you that it's your greatest
worth.
Because **you're more than what people see,**
you're a force in what they can't.

God isn't impressed by your filters.
He's moved by your faith.
He's not clapping for your angles; He's honoring your sacrifice.

So today, take back your power.
Not by doing more or showing more,

but by *surrendering more.*
Because obedience doesn't just make you powerful,
it makes you unstoppable.

Obedience Over Optics Prayer:

Lord,

I'm done chasing worth through what fades.

Let my beauty be bold, but let my obedience be what defines me.

I want to be the kind of woman who doesn't just look good, but lives

surrendered, walks in purpose, and answers Your voice with a holy yes.

Strip away what's surface. Strengthen what's sacred.

Let my power be in my obedience, every time.

In Jesus Name

Amen.

Song Reflection: "Make Room" by The Church Will Sing

Let this one be your anthem today.

"I will make room for You to do whatever You want to…"

Because there's nothing more beautiful than a woman fully yielded to Jesus.

That's what makes hell nervous.

Journal Prompts :

Where have you felt pressure to be more "attractive" instead of more obedient?

What's one way you've obeyed God that no one ever saw, but it changed everything?

Write this declaration:

"I am not just seen, I am sent. My obedience is my offering."

Day 15

Made for the Middle of the Fight

"Blessed be the Lord, my rock, who trains my
hands for war, and my fingers for battle." Psalms
144:1 (NASB)

This one's for the woman who didn't choose the fight
but keeps waking up in the middle of one.
You didn't ask for this battle.
You didn't go looking for the storm.

You weren't out here praying for pain or begging to be refined.
 If i am being honest here... i don't know a single soul who would be out here
requesting pain..I can do bad all by myself, I don't need to ask for help.
I've proven that time and time again..

But the war showed up anyway.
The attack came.
The enemy pressed in.
Life hit hard and didn't wait for you to be ready.
And still, **you're here.**
Still standing.
Still swinging.
Still showing up when everything in you wants to run.
And it's not because you're unshakable.
It's because **God trained you for this.**

You weren't built for comfort, you were built for *combat*.
You were made for the middle of the fight.
Where faith gets loud.
Where prayer gets fierce.
Where worship becomes warfare.

You don't fight like the world fights.
You fight with truth. With praise. With intercession.
With declarations that don't just shake earth, they *shake hell.*

You are not weak because you're in a battle.

You are in the battle because you're a threat.

The middle feels messy.
It feels like questions, exhaustion, and unanswered prayers.
But don't confuse the tension for a lack of calling.
God has never lost a war,
and He didn't put a warrior like you in this fight to lose.

Battlefield Prayer:

God,

I don't always understand the fight I'm in.

But I trust that if You've allowed me to face it,

You've equipped me to win it.

Train me in Your wisdom. Strengthen me with Your word.

Make me dangerous to darkness.

Let the middle of this mess be where I find You most.

And let every swing I take in faith be felt in the spirit.

I am not afraid of the fight, because

You fight through me.

In Jesus Name

Amen.

Song Reflection: "Battle Belongs" by Phil Wickham

Let this song blast while you lace up your armor.

"When I fight, I fight on my knees..."

You're not just fighting for victory; you're fighting *from* it.

God trusted you with the battlefield because He equipped you to win.

Journal Prompts :

What current "middle" are you fighting through?

How has God trained you, through past pain or present struggle,
to fight with faith?

Write this declaration:

"I wasn't made to run from the battle, I was built to rise in the middle of it."

Reflections

Weapon Inventory:
You picked up your sword.
You remembered your armor.
You prayed with authority.

Which weapon of warfare (Word, worship, prayer, fasting, rest, etc.)
hit deepest for you?

How did your posture change from passive to powerful?

What part of your fight are you most proud of?

Prompt :

Write a "Warrior's Resume." List out spiritual wins, surrendered places,

and every piece of armor you're choosing to wear daily.

Day 16

Heaven Doesn't Need You Perfect, Just Present

"Come to Me, all who are weary and burdened,
and I will give you rest.", Matthew 11:28 (NASB)

This one is a holy exhale...truth for the woman who's tired of performing,
striving, and trying to earn what Jesus already paid for.

You've spent a lot of time trying to get it right.

Trying to say the right prayers.
Do the right things.
Be the right version of a "strong Christian woman."
But can we be real for a minute?

God didn't ask you to be perfect.
As a matter of fact, He clearly states there is none perfect
He simply asked you to come.

Show up.
Messy.
Tired.
Questioning.
Still trying to forgive.
Still healing.
Still showing up with shaking hands and eyes swollen
from crying the night before.
Still uncertain of how to pray.
Insecure.
And He says that's enough.
He calls you beautiful.. even in your uncertainty.
He's not grading you.
He's not waiting for you to get your emotions under control
before He listens.
He doesn't need a polished version of you to work with.
He wants *the real you*, the one that's barely holding it
together
and came anyway.

Because presence is more powerful than performance.

You don't have to be perfect to be chosen.
You don't have to be strong to be used.
You don't have to have it all figured out to fall into His arms.
The lie says, "fix it first."
But grace says, **"Just come."**
If you're here, still breathing, still reaching, still whispering His name,
   you're already closer than you think.
 He sees your heart, he knows the questions, the imperfections and the unworthiness you feel.
He has seen it all and still asks you to come to Him,
To give Him your burdens, to lay down your confusion and to find serenity in His presence.

Come-As-You-Are Prayer:

My Jesus,
I've spent too long trying to earn what You already gave.
Trying to be enough when You've already called me loved.
I'm tired of performing. I just want to be present.
Meet me here, in the mess, in the in-between, in the quiet.
I don't bring perfection, but I bring my heart. And that's all You ever wanted.
In Jesus Name
Amen.

Song Reflection: "Come As You Are" by Crowder

Let this one break something open inside you.
"So lay down your burdens, lay down your shame..."
No more striving. No more masks.
You are welcome here. Just as you are

Journal Prompts :

Where have you been trying to "fix it" before you fully show up with God?

What version of perfection are you chasing that Jesus never asked for?

Write this reminder:

"Heaven isn't impressed with my performance; it delights in my presence."

Day 17

No One Else Gets to Name You

*"I will give you a new name that the Lord Himself
will give."*, Isaiah 62:2 (NLT)

LET'S GO RECLAIM EVERY stolen label and shut down every lie.
This one?
It's personal, powerful, and *holy ground* for
the woman who's ready to remember exactly who she is,
and **who gets to say so.**
You've been called a lot of things.
Too much.

Too sensitive.
Too bossy.
Too broken.
Too fat.
Too skinny.
Too ambitious.
Too shy.

Not enough.

Not holy enough.

Not pretty enough.

Not worthy enough.

You've worn names that didn't belong to you

and carried labels that never came from God.

 And maybe, somewhere deep down, you believed them.

Maybe you made those names your identity.

And now they echo in your mind when you walk into rooms,

raise your voice, or dare to dream.

 But here's what you need to know:

They don't get to name you.

Only God does.

And He calls you:

Daughter. Redeemed. Chosen.

Holy. Loved. Seen.

Set apart. Worthy. Warrior.

His.

 God never called you damaged.

He never called you forgotten.

He never labeled you based on what you did, or what was done

to you.

He named you before the pain.

He knew you before the lie.

And He still gets the final say.

 So today is your *name reclamation.*

You are not what they said.

You are not what you feared.

You are not who shame has tried to make you.

You are who Heaven says you are.
Period.

Name Reclaiming Prayer:

God,

I've carried names You never gave me.

I've believed voices that didn't sound like Yours.

But today, I silence every lie that tried to rename me.

I am not too much. I am not unworthy.

I am not a mistake.

I am Yours.

Rewrite my name with Your truth.

Let every other voice fall silent.

Only You get to speak into who I am.

Speak Lord, directly to my heart.

In Jesus Name

Amen.

Song Reflection: "I Am No Victim" by Kristene DiMarco

Let this anthem rise like a banner over every false label you've ever worn.

"I am who He says I am, and He is who He says He is."

This isn't just a song; it's a full-on identity reset.

Declare it. Weep with it. Dance with it.

Let it soundtrack the shedding of every name that was never yours to carry.

You are not a victim of your story.

You are a daughter of the King, named, known, and never mistaken.

Journal Prompts :

What names or labels have you carried that didn't come from God?

How have those names shaped the way you see yourself, and how can you
lay them down today?

Finish this declaration: *"I am not what they said. I am
_____."*

Day 18

Anointing Over Applause

"But when you give... do not let your left hand know what your right hand is doing, so that your giving will be in secret; and your Father who sees what is done in secret will reward you.", Matthew 6:3–4 (NASB)

...because you don't need a stage to be powerful, and you don't need applause to be anointed

There's a kind of power that never needs to be seen.
It doesn't need followers.
It doesn't need a platform.
It doesn't crave attention...it craves obedience.
And *that* kind of power?
That's called **anointing**.

There is only one place to receive that.
It's what makes a woman dangerous to the enemy,
even when no one else notices her.
It's what breaks chains in the unseen places.
It's what turns a whispered prayer into a supernatural
breakthrough.
It's what *heaven celebrates*, even when the world is silent.

Applause fades.
Likes disappear.
Crowds move on.
But anointing?
It stays. It multiplies. It marks you.

And sometimes, your most obedient yes will be the one no one
claps for.
The private surrender.
The behind-the-scenes obedience.
The silent act of sacrifice.
But God saw it.
God felt it.

God received it like worship.

Don't trade your oil for validation.

If you have to choose between applause and anointing,
always choose the one that can't be taken from you.
Because favor from people can open doors, but anointing tears
off hinges.

Prayer for Private Power:

Jesus,

I don't want to be impressive, I want to be effective.

Strip away every desire to be seen for what I do

instead of known for who I obey.

Make my secret place strong.

Let my anointing speak louder than my résumé.

I'd rather be anonymous in the world and approved in Heaven

than celebrated in culture and unknown in the Spirit.

So I choose the oil. I choose obedience.

Even if no one ever claps...I'll still say yes.

In Jesus Name

Amen.

Song Reflections "Nothing Else" by Cody Carnes

"I'm caught up in Your presence... I just want You."

When the applause fades and the lights are off, this song reminds

you what matters.

You don't want more attention; you want more of Him.

Journal Prompts :

Where have you sought validation instead of obedience?

What act of surrender or faithfulness are you being called to that *no one else will see, but God will?*

Finish this truth: *"My anointing matters more than* _____."

Day 19

Prayers That Punch Back

"The prayer of a righteous person is powerful and effective.", James 5:16 (NASB)

Let's go, warrior.
This one isn't soft, it's strategic.
Because some prayers aren't polite, they're powerful.

Prayer isn't a whisper into the void.
It's not a desperate shot in the dark.
It's not spiritual small talk or emotional therapy.
It's warfare.

And every time you open your mouth to pray,
you swing.

You punch back against every lie.
You counter every attack.
You speak truth into the atmosphere and **heaven responds**
The enemy hopes you never figure this out.
He wants you to believe your prayers are pointless, quiet,
passive.
But when you pray, especially when you *don't feel like it*,
you shift things in the spirit.
You may not see it yet.
You may not feel it.
But your prayers are **breaking ground, binding darkness,
and releasing power.**

Don't pray small when you serve a God who *shakes mountains.*
Don't pray weak when the same Spirit who raised Jesus
from the grave lives in you.

Pray like a daughter with divine authority.
Pray like you've got a whole army behind you, because you
do.

You've cried through it.
Now it's time to fight through it.
 You're not just surviving anymore.

You're standing.

You're speaking.

You're **punching back.**

Your prayers and anointing provide the perfect combination punch

for the knockout.

Prayer for Power in Prayer:

God,

Remind me that every time I pray, I wage war.

Teach me to pray with fire, with faith, and with full expectation.

No more polite prayers. No more passive agreement with fear.

Let my words carry weight. Let my petitions carry power.

I'm not just talking, I'm taking back territory.

In Jesus' name, I punch back.

Amen.

Song Reflections: "Talking to Jesus" by Elevation Worship & Maverick City

It starts simple but builds into a declaration of generational impact.

"*There's no wrong way to do it, Theres no bad time to start..* "

Your prayers aren't just for you, they're punching back for your children, your family, your future.

Journal Prompts :

What have you been praying about that feels like it's not moving?

How can you shift from praying out of desperation to praying with authority?

Write your own battle prayer for one area of your life where the enemy has been hitting hardest.

Day 20

She Isn't Intimidating, She's Anointed

"Now when they saw the boldness of Peter and John... they recognized them as having been with Jesus.", Acts 4:13 (NASB)

It's not about arrogance, it's about *alignment.*
You're not too much, too bold, or too intense...
You're just anointed. And that changes everything.
 They'll say you're too much.
Too confident.
Too opinionated.

Too intense.
Too spiritual.
Too loud.
Too focused.

And when their comfort is challenged by your clarity,
they'll call it "intimidating."
 But girl, **you're not intimidating. You're anointed.**
And people who haven't seen what you've fought through...
who haven't carried what you've carried...
who haven't stayed when it would've been easier to run
they *won't always know what to do with you.*

But that's not your problem.

Your job isn't to shrink so others can stay comfortable.
Your job is to **walk in the power of your assignment**
like the daughter of God you are.
Because you didn't come this far just to start doubting your
presence now.

You've been refined by fire.
You've got oil that came from crushing.
You've got boldness that was birthed in the secret place.
And Heaven has marked you.

So don't apologize for your voice.
Don't down play your discernment.
Don't silence your spiritual confidence.

You don't need to be liked to be *legitimately called.*

They might say it's "too much."

But in the spirit?
It's exactly what this world needs

Prayer for Unapologetic Anointing:

Jesus,

I'm done dimming what You've lit inside me.

If my boldness shakes the room, let it be because You walked in with me.

Let me walk in the fullness of my anointing,

not to impress, not to intimidate, but to obey.

I won't shrink. I won't apologize.

I am anointed, not arrogant.

And I'm showing up in the power of Your name.

In Jesus Name

Amen.

Song Reflections: "Send Me" by Jenn Johnson & Bethel Music

If you've ever questioned why you're built the way you are, this song answers it:

*"If You're looking for someone to go, **I'm ready.**"*

That fire in you? **It's on purpose.**

Journal Prompts :

Have you ever been told you were "too much"?
How did that shape how you show up?

What have you been toning down that God wants to turn *all the way up?*

Finish this with fire: *"I'm not intimidating, I'm _____."*

Reflections

My Voice Wrecks the Silence

You learned your prayers aren't whispers, they're *weapons*.
You don't just speak, you *shift atmospheres*.

What lie has the enemy fed you about your voice or your prayers?

Where have you seen your words carry weight in the spirit realm lately?

Prompt :

Write 3 spiritual declarations that you will keep speaking out loud over your life.

Day 21

When She Worships in the Dark

"Though the fig tree should not blossom... yet I will rejoice in the Lord; I will take joy in the God of my salvation.", Habakkuk 3:17–18 (NASB)

...because this one is sacred.
It's for the woman who shows up to worship
while her heart is breaking,
because even when it's dark, **she still knows who her God is.**

Anybody can worship when life is good.

When doors are opening.
When prayers are answered.
When the sun is shining, and your heart feels whole.
But what about when everything hurts?

When nothing makes sense?

When the silence is deafening and the only light

you see is the kind you *used* to feel?

That's where real worship begins.

Worship in the dark is war.

Worship in the dark is personal.

It's the love song you sing to Jesus, and it's his answer back.

It's holy defiance.

It's saying, "I don't understand You right now, but I still trust

You."

It's praising with a cracked voice and shaking hands.

It's lifting your arms when all you want to do is collapse.

It's declaring truth when the facts are still breaking your

heart.

And that kind of worship?

Hell hates it.

Hell hates it because Heaven moves when you worship in the

dark.

Chains break when you worship in the dark.

Addictions cease when you worship in the dark.

Healing happens when you worship in the dark.

Jesus speaks when you worship in the dark.

Victory is secured when you worship in the dark.

It brings about a breakthrough, you enter beyond the gates,

behind

the veil, past the inner courts, to that place where vulnerability

sits,

and love is poured out.

Because it means the enemy didn't win.
It means grief didn't shut you down.
It means your pain didn't steal your praise.
It means you're still standing in faith, even if you're
standing in the dark.

Don't wait for the light to sing.
Let your worship be the thing that brings the light in.

Prayer for the Midnight Praise:

God,
This praise costs me something.
It's not pretty. It's not polished. It's not loud.
But it's *real*. And You're still worthy of it.
I don't see the answer yet, but I still know You're good.
Even in the dark, I will sing.
Even in the silence, I will worship.
Because this isn't just a song. It's a weapon.
And I choose to wield it.
In Jesus Name
Amen.

Song Reflections "Do it Again" by Elevation Worship

This one doesn't just meet you in the wilderness, it walks with you through it.

"Your promise still stands, Great is Your faithfulness."

It's not about performance. It's about *presence.*

And your praise in the dark? It's setting things free.

Journal Prompts :

What is your heart grieving or fighting through right now?

What truth do you *know* even when you don't feel it?

Write this down as your battle cry: *"Even here, even now, I will worship."*

Day 22

Rest Is a Weapon, Too

"In peace I will lie down and sleep, for You alone, Lord, have me dwell in safety.", Psalms 4:8 (NASB)

...because this one is a whole revelation for the woman who's been taught to hustle like it's holy.
But today? We trade burnout for **battle-ready rest.**

You've been taught that movement equals progress.
That busy equals worthy.

That if you're not pushing, producing, or posting, you're falling behind.

But Heaven doesn't operate on hustle.

Heaven operates on rest.

To rest is so much more than stopping. more than a nap, more than silence

or stillness.

To rest is to release.. to let go of the pressure to perform, to prove, to produce.

Its surrender in motion, the radical act of saying, "God I trust you to hold,

what i can't carry."

Not laziness. Not avoidance.

Rest. As in trust.

As in surrender.

As in "God's got this."

Rest means putting down the outcome, the approval, the timeline.

We burn out trying to micromanage things only God can truly fix.

Because true rest isn't doing nothing.

It's doing *only what God asked* and trusting Him with the rest.

You're allowed to rest *without guilt.*

You're allowed to pause and not fall apart.

You're allowed to sleep and not lose ground.

Rest is warfare when you're living in a world addicted to exhaustion.

Even warriors retreat.
Even Jesus *slept on a boat in a storm.*
Even angels came and ministered to Him when He was weak.

So if the Son of God rested,
what makes you think your burnout makes you holy?

Sis, put the cape down.
You are not the Savior, Jesus is.
You're not lazy because you said no.
You're not selfish because you took a nap.
You're not falling behind; you're finally walking in rhythm
with the Spirit.

And that?
That's a weapon the enemy can't stand.

Prayer of Holy Rest:

God,

I lay down my need to be everything, fix everything, do everything.

Remind me that rest is not weakness, it's wisdom.

Give me peace that silences pressure.

Help me pause without panic.

And let my stillness shout to the world:

"I trust You more than I trust my own hustle."

In Jesus Name

Amen.

Song Reflections "Quiet"by Elevation Rhythm

This one speaks to the swirl of anxiety that creeps into every moment of stillness.

"I don't need to know what comes next. Tomorrow's in Your hands..."

Let it hush the hustle.

Journal Prompts :

What lies have you believed about rest, productivity, and your worth?

What would change if you believed that rest was actually part of
your obedience?

Write this declaration: *"Rest is not falling behind. It's walking in trust."*

Day 23

Fasting Isn't Just for Saints, It's for Fighters

"Is this not the fast that I choose: to release the bonds of wickedness, to undo the ropes of the yoke, to let the oppressed go free...?", Isaiah 58:6 (NASB)

This one is for the women who are hungry for more than comfort,

the ones who are done just surviving and ready to fight with
fire and focus.

Fasting has a reputation.
We picture saints in silence.
Holy people who wakeup at 5 a.m., skip breakfast, and
float through temptation with angelic patience.

But what if fasting isn't just for saints?
What if it's for fighters?

Because fasting is war.

It's the decision to trade physical comfort for spiritual clarity.

It's saying, *"I want breakthrough more than I want brunch."*

It's a full-body, soul-deep cry that says:

"God, I need You more than anything else I could consume right now."

Fasting doesn't impress God.

It doesn't manipulate Him.

But it *does* do this:

It silences distractions.

It weakens the flesh.

It sharpens your hearing.

It multiplies your power.

Fasting clears the fog and strengthens the fight.

It's not about starving, it's about aligning.

It's laying down what your body craves so your spirit can rise.

Don't fast to perform.

Fast to pursue.

Because something happens in the spirit when you lay down the natural, **something shifts.**

Something breaks.

Something moves.

Think about it..

Moses fasted and met with God face to face.

Esther fasted for courage and favor.

Jesus fasted and resisted the enemy.

The early church fasted before any major decisions.

Prayer for Focused Fire:

Jesus,

I want to want You more.

More than comfort. More than caffeine.

More than anything that numbs or fills.

Teach me how to fast, not out of religion, but out of hunger.

Show me what You want to break off.

What You want to reveal.

I don't want a shallow life. I want the deep.

The heavy. The holy. Let fasting be my fight song.

Let surrender be my strength.

In Jesus Name

Amen.

Song Reflections: "Fresh Fire" by Maverick City Music

Fasting is fuel. And this song?

It's what you play when you want to *burn again.*

"I wanna burn for You..."

Turn it up and let it refine you.

Journal Prompts:

What's been fogging your focus lately? What needs to be laid down?

How could fasting become part of your spiritual warfare, not just your tradition?

Write this declaration: *"I fast because I'm not powerless, I'm preparing."*

Day 24

Don't Wait to Be Brave

"Have I not commanded you? Be strong and courageous! Do not be terrified nor dismayed, for the Lord your God is with you wherever you go.",
Joshua 1:9 (NASB)

Sometimes we think bravery has to wait.

Wait until we are move healed.

Wait until we are not afraid.

Wait until we are over it, until we have processed it, until we feel strong.

You keep waiting for confidence to hit.

To feel bold enough.

Qualified enough.

Ready enough.

You keep praying for confirmation, for clarity, for *courage to finally rise up.*

But what if it's not about waiting for bravery to *arrive?*

What if you were made to go scared?

Bravery rarely feels like readiness.

It feels like trembling hands choosing to reach anyway.

It feels like a voice that shakes but still speaks

Because bravery doesn't always roar.

Sometimes it whispers, *"I'm still going."*

It gets in the car even when your hands are shaking.

It speaks up even when your voice is cracking.

It shows up, heart

racing, stomach flipping, *but feet still moving.*

You don't have to feel brave to be brave.

You just have to go with God.

That fear? It's loud.

But obedience is louder.

And when you take that first step in trembling faith,

He meets you there, everytime.

Don't wait until the butterflies leave.

Don't wait until the imposter syndrome fades.

Don't wait until you feel "spiritual enough," "wise enough," "healed enough."

Go now.

Speak now.

Write the thing.

Apply for the role.

Start the ministry.

Leave what's killing your spirit.

Be bold, before you feel it.

Because bravery isn't a feeling.

It's a decision to trust that He goes before you.

Prayer for Bold Obedience:

God,

I'm done waiting to feel brave.

You didn't ask for perfection; you asked for my yes.

So here it is. Even with the fear. Even with the doubt.

Even with trembling hands.

I trust You more than I trust my nerves.

Walk with me. War through me.

Make me dangerous to every room fear told me I couldn't enter.

In Jesus Name

Amen.

Song Reflections "Brave"by Amanda Cook

Not loud bravery. Not forced.

Just *honest, spirit-led courage.*

Let it wash over you as a permission slip to walk forward, exactly as you are.

Journal Prompts :

What have you been waiting to do until you "feel" ready?

What would it look like to move now, in obedience, not just in confidence?

Declare this in faith: *"I'm not fearless, but I'm moving. And that's enough."*

Day 25

Your Armor Still Fits

*"Put on the full armor of God, so that you will
be able to stand firm against the schemes of the
devil.",* Ephesians 6:11 (NASB)

...because this one isn't just a reminder. It's a **battle cry.**

You've been hit.
Hard.

Life didn't just throw punches;
it threw full-on uppercuts.
You've questioned your strength.
You've wondered if you were still built for this.
And somewhere along the way, you started to believe maybe your time was up.
That someone else was better equipped.
That your armor didn't fit anymore.
But can I remind you of something?
The fight didn't change your calling.
And your wounds didn't strip your authority.
You are still a warrior.
Still dangerous.
Still covered.
And your armor still fits.
Yes, you may have dents in your shield.
Yes, you may be dragging your sword.
Yes, the helmet may feel heavy right now.
But it's *still yours*.
And it *still works*.

God didn't give you temporary strength.
He gave you eternal armor.
The kind that doesn't expire.
The kind that doesn't fall off when you fall down
So today? Suit up again.
Not because you feel like it, but because *you were built for this*.
You don't have to go looking for new tools.

You already have what you need to stand.

The enemy wants you to forget your weapons.

He wants you to question your strength.

He wants you to walk into battle insecure.

But girl, your belt is truth.

Your shield is faith.

Your shoes? Peace.

Your helmet? Salvation.

Your sword? The Word of God.

And your stance? Already victorious.

You're not too broken.

You're not too late.

You're not too anything.

You're armed. And you're still called.

Prayer for the Fully Armored Woman:

Lord,

Sometimes I forget how dangerous I really am.

Remind me that I don't fight alone, and I don't fight unarmed.

Every piece of armor still fits me.

Even with the bruises. Even with the questions. Even when I'm tired.

Let me pick up my shield, raise my sword, and stand tall in who

You've called me to be.

Because the fight isn't over, and neither am I.

In Jesus Name

Amen.

Song Reflections: "Champion"by Bethel Music (feat. Dante Bowe)

This is your soundtrack for standing back up.

"You are my Champion / giants fall when You stand..."

Let this song remind you:

you're not fighting for victory; you're fighting *from* it.

Journal Prompts :

What piece of spiritual armor have you laid down or forgotten about lately?

How does it change your posture to remember that you are *already equipped*?

Declare this over yourself:
"I may be weary, but my armor still fits, and I still fight."

Reflections

Worship Is My Warfare

You discovered your worship
is not background noise,
it's a battleground.

How did your view of worship shift from music to *a weapon?*

What dark moment did you choose to praise your way through anyway?

What happens to your spirit when you worship before the breakthrough?

Prompt :

Write a worship declaration starting with: "When I raise my voice, I..."

Day 26

Her Worship Is a Weapon

"Let God arise, let His enemies be scattered...",
Psalms 68:1 (NASB)

She's not just singing,
she's swinging.
Worship isn't weak.
It's war.
When she raises her hands,
Heaven stands behind her.

There is something wild and holy that happens
when a woman worships through the war.
When she lifts her voice with trembling hands and tired eyes,
she's not just surviving,
she's fighting.
Worship isn't a warm-up.
It's not a passive act.
It's a declaration of defiance in the face of every lie,
every fear, and every enemy whisper that told her she wouldn't
make it.
Because when the enemy comes for your peace, your purpose,
your identity,
and your joy, you don't just fight back with fists.
You fight with FAITH.
And worship is faith in motion.
Hell hates when you worship because it means you remember
who's really in charge.
You're not singing _**for**_ victory; you're singing _**from**_ it.
Consider Paul and Silas worshiping from their prison cell,
worshiping in
chains. Not after the miracle, but in the midnight hour,
in the middle of their pain.
God met them right there, not in comfort, but in the fight.
Because worship tells the darkness,
"You can take a lot from me, but you can't take my song."
You're calling Heaven into your situation with every lyric
and lifting your head when the weight of the world wants it
down.

Girl, when you worship, God rises.

And when He rises, your enemies scatter.

So, lift your voice. Even if it shakes.

Raise your hands. Even if they feel heavy.

Let the tears fall. Let your soul sing.

Because **this praise? It's warfare.**

And you don't fight like the world fights.

You fight likeHeaven.

Warfare Prayer:

God,

Let my worship be my war cry.

When fear comes knocking, let praise be what opens the door.

I declare that no weapon formed against me will prosper,

because You, the King of Glory, fight on my behalf.

Even in the middle of the battle, especially there, I will lift You up.

Let my praise shake the gates of hell and remind the enemy who I belong to.

In Jesus Name

Amen.

Song Reflection: "Raise a Hallelujah" by Bethel Music

"Sing louder than the unbelief."

Louder than the fear. Louder than the enemy.

Turn this song up and remind your heart that **praise isn't a feeling,**

it's a choice.

You're not just singing; you're shifting atmospheres

Journal Prompts :

What battles have tried to silence your worship lately?

What happens to your spirit when you worship
even when you don't feel like it?

Write a declaration you can speak over yourself before or
during worship.

Day 27

When She Speaks, Heaven Moves

"Death and life are in the power of the tongue..."
, Proverbs 18:21

She doesn't need a platform.
She needs her voice.
Her prayers rearrange atmospheres.
Her words break chains.

There's something dangerous about a woman who knows
the weight of her words.

Not because she's loud, but because, she's *sure*.

Sure of who she is.

Sure of who her God is.

And absolutely sure that when she speaks in alignment with Heaven,

things move.

The enemy would love nothing more than to silence you.

To convince you that your voice doesn't carry authority.

To muzzle your prayers,

dull your declarations,

and keep you second-guessing instead of prophesying.

But let me remind you:

Your words are not soft. They are sharp.

Your prayers are not passive. They are powerful.

Your voice is not a whisper in the wind. It is a roar in the Spirit.

When you speak the name of Jesus, hell trembles.

When you declare God's promises over your life, angels are dispatched.

When you refuse to agree with fear, anxiety, shame, or defeat,

you are canceling the contracts the enemy tried to place over your future.

So speak, daughter.

Speak healing over your home.

Speak life over your body.

Speak freedom over your family.
Speak like the gates of hell are listening,
because they are.

Fire Prayer:

Jesus,
I refuse to let my voice go silent when
You've given me the power to speak life.
Teach me to pray with precision, declare with boldness,
and never water down the truth of Your Word.
Let everything I speak echo the power of Heaven,
and shut down the lies of the enemy the moment they try to
rise.
I will not be silenced. I will not be small.
I speak with holy fire. I speak with divine authority.
In Jesus' mighty name,
Amen.

Song Reflection: "I Speak Jesus" by Here Be Lions

Let this be your anthem today.
Declare His name over fear, anxiety, addiction, your family,
your future.
**There'spower in your voice, not because of you,
but because of who you're speaking.**
And when you speak Jesus, **chains break.**

Journal Prompts :

What lie has tried to silence your voice or minimize your prayers?

Write 3 declarations of truth over your life today, use scripture to back them.

When you speak, what do you want the spiritual realm to hear?

Day 28

She's Got Oil and Fire

"But the wise took oil in their vessels with their lamps.", Matthew 25:4(NASB)

She stays ready, anointed, lit, filled.
She doesn't wait for a fight to prepare.
She *carries fire* in her spirit and oil in her lamp.
Stay full.
Stay dangerous.

Some women wait for the battle to find them before they get ready.

But not her.

She stays ready.

Because she knows that oil runs deep, and fire doesn't fall on empty altars.

She's the kind of woman who's been through too much to live casually.

She's learned how to refill when no one's watching.

She's learned how to keep her lamp burning
in rooms where others lost their light.

And even when the night is long, **she's got oil and fire.**

Oil comes from crushing,
from seasons where she didn't know if she'd make it,
from prayers prayed through gritted teeth,
from moments she praised with tears in her eyes
and fists still clenched.

And fire?

That's not just energy, it's anointing.

It's the spark of the Spirit alive in her bones.

It's the holy glow of someone who's been in the presence of God
and refuses to live in shadows anymore.

You don't have to beg for fire.

You just have to stay full of oil.

That means staying close to Him.

Filling up daily.
Pouring it out when He asks.
And refusing to live on yesterday's encounter.

You're not burnt out; you just need to refill.
And when you do?
You'll burn brighter than anything that ever tried to dim you.

Refilling Prayer:

God,
Make me a vessel You can trust with the fire.
Let me carry oil with wisdom, not pride.
Remind me that my power doesn't come from hype or hustle, but
from intimacy with You.
Keep me filled, keep me faithful, and keep me burning.
Let my flame never flicker because I forgot where the oil comes from.
Fill me up again, Lord, until I overflow.
Amen.

Song Reflection: "Fresh Wind" by Hillsong Worship

Let this song be your cry:

"We need a fresh wind, the fragrance of Heaven / Pour Your Spirit out."

You don't need to run on fumes. You were made to overflow.

Ask for oil.

Expect fire.

Journal Prompts :

What season of crushing produced the most oil in your life?

What helps you refill spiritually when you feel dry or tired?

Where in your life do you need to reignite the fire of faith and devotion?

Day 29

The Devil Regrets Messing with Her

"You intended to harm me, but God intended it for good to accomplish what is now being done...",
Genesis 50:20 (NASB)

Every attack?
A setup for glory.
Every hit she took?
A prophecy she's still standing.
He tried to take her out, but she got louder.
Hell underestimated the wrong girl.

He thought it would break her.

The loss. The betrayal. The isolation. The storm.

He whispered that this would be the thing to take her out.

But instead, it lit her up.

She didn't just survive the attack,
she rose with fire in her eyes and prophecy in her lungs.

Every hit from the enemy only sharpened her discernment.
Every valley deepened her worship.
Every lie made her hunger for truth even more.

And now?
The devil regrets ever messing with her.
Because the ground he tried to bury her in?
God turned it into **soil for revival**.
She's not who she used to be.
She's dangerous now.
Because she knows too much.
She's seen God turn ashes into glory.
She's seen miracles grow out of mourning.
She's learned how to praise in prison,
prophesy in pain,
and walk in power even with a limp.

You are that woman.
You are the living, breathing proof that hell can't stop what
Heaven has ordained.
So stop waiting to feel worthy.
Start walking like someone who made the devil regret the day
he came for your calling.

Redemption Prayer:

God,
Thank You for turning every weapon into a testimony.
Thank You for using the very things meant to break me
to build me into someone more bold, more healed,
and more on fire than ever.
I declare that the enemy's plans have failed.
His threats are empty. His grip is broken.
And I am still here, not just breathing, but **burning** with
purpose.
In Jesus Name
Amen.

Song Reflection: "See a Victory" by Elevation Worship

Let this be your anthem:
*"You take what the enemy meant for evil and You turn it for
good."*
It's not just a lyric. It's your life.
**Worship like someonewho walked through hell and
came out carrying Heaven.**

Journal Prompts :

What attack did you think would take you out, but God used it to raise you up?

How has your relationship with Jesus grown through pain?

What do you want the enemy to regret every time he hears your name?

Day 30

She Knows Whose Name She Carries

*"So that at the name of Jesus every knee will bow,
of those who are in heaven and on earth and under
the earth.",* Philippians 2:10 (NASB)

You carry the name that breaks every chain.
 There's a reason hell trembles when she prays.
It's not because she's loud.
Not because she's perfect.
Not even because she's fearless.
It's because **she knows whose name she carries.**

And she trusts that when she calls on His name, all things must bow.

She's not speaking on her own behalf; she's carrying royal authority.

Every time she says, "in Jesus' name,"

she is invoking **the name that split graves, shattered chains, and silenced death itself**

That name isn't a tagline, it's her weapon.

Her armor.

Her access point.

Her covering.

Her rescue.

And she doesn't just wear it on Sundays, **she walks in it daily.**

When she prays for her family, Heaven listens.

When she steps into chaos, peace comes with her.

When she whispers that name in the middle of the night,

demons scatter and angels stand guard.

Because **Jesus isn't just a name. He's her power source.**

She may be underestimated.

She may be overlooked.

But she's *never* outnumbered.

Because the King of Kings backs her every step.

She doesn't need to prove herself.

She just needs to remember:

the name she carries is enough.

Final Prayer:

Jesus,

Your name is my refuge, my authority, my weapon, and my worship.

Let me never treat it like punctuation, let me carry it like power.

When I speak it, may chains break.

When I whisper it, may peace rise.

When I stand in it, may darkness flee.

I belong to You. I bear Your name.

And that changes *everything*.

In Jesus Name

Amen.

Song Reflection: "Jesus"by Chris Tomlin
(or "There'sJust Something About That Name" by Gaither Vocal Band)

Let this be your reminder. Simple. Powerful.

There's no name like Jesus.

And the same name that raised the dead now lives on your lips.

Say it often. Say it boldly. Say it with everything you are

Journal Prompts :

How have you seen the power of Jesus' name in your own life?

What would change if you walked every day fully aware of whose
name you carry?

Write a declaration of who you are *because* of who He is.

Reflections

**Holy Identity
Check-In:**

Who am I *really* in Christ?

Where have I been living small when God's called me to rise up?

What lies do I need to lay down once and for all?

Reignite the Fight:

What area of my life needs fire again?

Where have I been silenced, and what would it look like to speak boldly again?

What scripture is my go-to battle cry?

My Voice, My Weapon:

What truth can I speak over myself daily?

How can I walk in authority without becoming hard or performative?

What would I tell another woman who forgot how dangerous she is in Jesus?

Bonus Prompt: Spiritual Debrief with God

"God, what are You proud of ,in me, from these 30 days?"
Then just listen. Write what you sense.
Even if it feels small. Even if you cry through it.
Let Him speak back.

She Never Fights Alone

THERE'S A BATTLE IN this world for your voice.

Your calling. Your mind. Your peace.

But what the enemy underestimated is **who you belong to.**

You're not just a woman of faith; you're a **force of Heaven.**

Your worship is warfare.

Your prayers are declarations.

Your obedience is a threat to hell.

And your identity? **Dangerous in the hands of God.**

These last thirty days weren't just words on a page.

They were a holy reminder:

You don't need to wait to be brave. You already are.

You don't need to find your power. You already carry His.

You don't need to be rescued. You've already been called.

So, keep fighting like Heaven.

Because the enemy may come at you like a flood,

but baby, **you know how to lift a standard.**

Heaven has your back. Jesus is your banner.

And fear doesn't get the final say.

Prayer for the One Who Finished the Fight

Jesus,

She made it.

She showed up, somedays on fire, some days in ashes,

but she showed up.

She peeled back the layers of fear, shame, and doubt.

She faced the lies. She spoke truth. She picked up her sword

again.

And now, standing on the other side of 30 days,

she may not feel "finished,"

but she is **forever changed.**

So I pray blessings on her now.

Not with comfort, but with *clarity.*

Not with ease, but with *eternal fire.*

Not with applause, but with *anointing that outlasts storms.*

May she remember that strength isn't in striving,

it's in surrender.

That rest is not retreat,

it's warfare in rhythm with Heaven.
And that worship,even when whispered through tears,
shakes hell in ways she will never fully see.
God, let her never again believe she is too much or not enough.
Let her never again give the enemy a louder voice than Your
Spirit.
Let her walk into every room as a woman who *knows Whose she*
is.
Let her pray with fire.
Let her love with holy boldness.
Let her speak life even in deserts.
Let her rise even with trembling hands.
And let this not be the end,
but the beginning of her fiercest, most Spirit-led season yet.
She doesn't just fight like heaven.
She *belongs* to Heaven.
And the gates of hell will never know peace again.
In Jesus' undefeated, all-powerful name,
Amen.

Grateful...

*To the ones who fight beside me with heaven in their hearts:
my beautiful children, my cherished best friends, and every
prayer warrior woman whose faith thunders like a war drum.
You are a living legacy of courage and grace. I see heaven's
light in your eyes and a warrior's fire in your souls, and I am
fiercely grateful for each of you.*

*And to the MIGHTY women of prayer who intercede like
warriors. I stand in awe of you. You are the secret army
that causes heaven to roar and hell to shudder. Tori Jones,
Tracy Matherly, Jamie Cantrell, Christie Hudman, Niki
Chandler , Kay McDaniel, Darci Dyer, Billie Jean Hayes,
Holly Jones, and Toni Roberson-you are life saving and life
speaking, the warriors I turn to when the battle rages on. My
family no matter how far apart we are. Thank you.*

*I didn't always have a relationship with Jesus. I had friends
who prayed fiercely for me (even when i didn't want it-
Thank you Holly) ... and they never stopped. I truly met*

Jesus for the first time in an elementary school cafeteria. I went to watch what I thought would be a spectacle, but as it turned out... It was a life changing miracle. In those quiet moments when a family was formed in a small church, in an even smaller town. I had so many questions, so many misgivings about what I was seeing, hearing and feeling. But God... He showed up every single time, answering all the questions, quieting all the fears. Showing me Whose I was. So, this is for my Pathway Fellowship family. Thank you for lighting my path and showing me what true worship looks like.

Shellie of the Isles....